A Lifetime's Weather

Its Highs and Lows

by Ian Lyall

A Lifetime's Weather

Its Highs and Lows

by Ian Lyall

Published by lulu.com

ISBN: 978-1-326-55396-8

FOREWORD

As I write this, I am approaching my 80th Birthday and aware that I am sitting on a record of weather in Newark-on-Trent in the UK, I feel it timely to put the record- or at least its highs and lows in the public domain

So, I have gone through that record and extracted what is, if you will, a chronicle of Newark-on-Trent's weather since 1951. The 'highs' and 'lows' are those of temperature rainfall, fog and frost snow and thunder by the year and also by the season. I do also make note of some of the more memorable weather events. Climate change is also a matter for brief comment, especially with the suspicion that the rate of warming is on the rise.

I hasten to add that I look forward to continuing recording our weather!

**I have a weather site at http://newarkweather.lyall-web.co.uk/mobile/

CONTENTS

1. A sixty-year Chronicle for 1951-2015

January

5th 1956 Maximum 56F (13.6C)
5th 1983 Maximum 13.8C

7th 1970 Minimum -9.9C
This was a cold January with the mildest day only reaching 8.7C on the 12th

8th 1992 daily rainfall of 27.7mm

9th 1998 Maximum 13.2C
9th Record 15.1C. The following night minimum at 13.1C was a record for January

10th 1968 Minimum -8,8C

12th 2007 Maximum 13.9C

13th 1987 Record cold of -16.1C (3.0F). The minimum actually occurred during the evening of the 12th

14th 1982 Minimum -14.0C; at the time a record, and the second coldest night in the record

15th 1954 Maximum 56F (13.6C)

16th 1993 Maximum 14.0C

17th 1985 Minimum -9.9C

18th 1955 Minimum 18F (-7.3C)

21st 1990 Maximum 13.4C in one of the mildest Januaries with a monthly minimum -1.7C on the 7th. There were only 2 air frosts and no snow was observed

22nd 1969 Maximum 12.7C
This was a very mild January, when the -2.2C on the 22nd was the coldest night

23rd 1963 Minimum 11F (-11.6C)
1962-3 was the coldest winter of the record: in fact it had the lowest CET since 1740. The most severe spell was from 21-25 January. Just as it seemed the severe cold might be ameliorating, a fresh burst of easterly winds behind a deepening low which plunged south across the country brought heavy snowfall on the 21st. The 22nd was brilliantly sunny with a bitter wind. The following night under clear skies the coldest night of the winter (11F, -11.6C) followed and despite sunny skies the day following could only reach 24F (-4.4C). Fog formation restricted the overnight low to 13F (-10.6C) but fog held the maximum to a perishing 21F (-5.6C). Thereafter temperatures began a slow recovery

28th 1979 Minimum -12.2C; a new record during the second coldest January

30th 1975 Maximum 13.3C; at the time a record high for January

31st 2000 Maximum 13.2C
31st 1972 Minimum -10.2C

February

1st 1987 Minimum -7.7C

2nd 1956 Minimum 16F (-9.0C)
2nd 2002 Maximum 14.7C

3rd 2004 Maximum 16.4C, unusual for so early

5th 1963 Minimum 15F (-9.4C) during the coldest February on record

10th 1986 Minimum -10.1C during a snowy month with snow lying on 17 days

11th 2011 Minimum -10.1C

12th 1985 Minimum -12.2C
12th 1998 Maximum 15.5C

13th 1969 Minimum -10.4C

14th 1991 Minimum -10.0C

15th 1979 Minimum -5.8C not exceptional, but in the middle of a very severe and snowy winter. 1978-79 was one of the snowiest winters of the record (although less so than 1946-47). The heaviest fall occurred on 14 February. Newark received 6 inches level snow and accompanying strong winds led to severe drifting. Many villages around Newark were cut off for several days. The ferocity of the storm can be adjudged by the fact that for many hours falling snow reduced visibility to less than 100m. The day maximum was -2.7C

21st 1961 Minimum 34F (1.1C), the lowest in a frost-free month

22nd 1953 Maximum 58F (14.5C)

23rd 1990 Maximum 18.3C, record for February

23rd 1991 Maximum 15.4C

23rd 2010 Maximum 16.4C

25th 1980 A wet day with 22.3mm rain

26th 1976 Maximum 15.2C

27th 1987 Maximum 14.8C

28th 1955 Record cold February night at the end of the month: 13F (-10.5C)

28th 1959 Maximum 62F (16.7C), for many years a record for February

29th 1960 Maximum 61F (16.1C)

March

1st 1955 Minimum 23F (-5.0C)

2nd 1954 Minimum 20F (-6.7C)
2nd 1965 Minimum 14F (-10.0C), the record low for March

3rd 1986 Minimum -7.8C
3rd 2006 Minimum -51C: the coldest night of the winter

6th 1982 Rainfall 25.0mm

7th 1969 Minimum -6.1C during the coldest March on record; the maximum was 13.2C on 31st

9th 1970 Minimum -7.0C
9th 1999 Maximum 19.0C

15th 1993 Maximum 19.0C

16th 1979 Rainfall 22.3mm

18th 1962 Minimum 23F (-6.7C)
18th 1985 Minimum -6.8C
18th 1990 Maximum 21.2C
18th 2005 Maximum 18.8C

20th Maximum 20.0C

21st 1967 Maximum 17.3C

25th 1953 Maximum 66F (18.9C)

27th 1989 Maximum 18.4C

28th 2012 Maximum 19.6C

29th 1965 Maximum 74F (23.4C), record high for March (both high and low in the same month.

 At the end of a month of contrasts (It began with harsh frosts-down on the 2nd to 14F (-10C) and then a more changeable period, pressure rose in an open warm sector on the 28th. The night following fell to just 35F (1.4C). But with unbroken sunshine and a low-level inversion there was an unprecedented rise in temperature to reach 74F (23.4C)- a March record.

29th 1968 Maximum 22.2C

29th 2002 Maximum 18.9C

30th 1998 Maximum 18.0C

April

1st 1967 Minimum -5.2C, at the time record cold for April

2nd 1970 Minimum -3.3C

3rd 1969 Minimum-3.4C
3rd 1983 Minimum -3.0C
3rd 1984 Minimum -5.4C
3rd 2000 Rainfall 24.2mm, falling as sleet/wet snow

9th 1973 Minimum -3.1C
9th 1977 Minimum -3.5C

10th 1975 Minimum -3.0C

11th 1971 Minimum -1.9C
11th 1978 Minimum -3.0C
11th 1985 Rainfall 21.7mm

16th 1980 Maximum 23.0C
16th 2003 Maximum 24.8C

20th 1968 Record frost for April, minimum -6.5C
20th 1981 Rainfall 20.1mm
20th 2012 Rainfall 22.4mm

21st 1984 Maximum 22.9C
21st 1996 Maximum 23.4C

23rd 2011 Record maximum of 25.8C

24th 1971 Rainfall 28.9mm on 24th

24th 1988 Minimum -2.1C

27th 2010 Maximum 22.9C

29th 1994 Maximum 23.3C

30th 1966 Maximum 75F (23.9C), at the time record warmth for April
30th 1976 Minimum -3.3C
30th 1990 Maximum 25.0C, new record for April

May

1st 1951 Minimum 34F (1.1C)

2nd 1965 Minimum 33F (0.6C)

3rd 1967 Minimum -2.8C, record lowest in May-after snow the previous evening
3rd 1971 Minimum -1.0C
3rd 1976 Minimum -0.2C

5th 1979 Minimum -2.1C
5th 1990 Maximum 26.9C; part of a five day spell 80F+

7th 2011 Rainfall 24.7mm

9th 1980 Minimum -1.9C

10th 1959 Maximum 80F (26.6C), before one of the hottest summers on record

11th 1967 Maximum 26.7C
11th 2003 Maximum 27.1C

12th 1979 Maximum 25.5C

14th 1965 Maximum 85F (29.4C), record hottest in May for many years.
14th 1966 Minimum 31F (-0.6C)
14th 1985 Rainfall 26.1mm
14th 1991 Maximum 27.1C

17th 1955 An exceptional day when snow fell

18th 1956 Minimum 34F (1.1C)

19th 1968 Minimum 1.2C
19th 2013 Maximum 27.2C

23rd 1989 Maximum 28.6C
23rd 2010 Record May heat at 30.7C

25th 1953 Maximum 83F (28.4C), for many years the May record

26th 2000 Rainfall 24.2mm.
26th 2009 Maximum 27.9C

28th 2012 Maximum 30.4C. This was the hottest day of the year

31st 1975 Minimum -0.5C: exceptional for end of May
31st 1978 Maximum 28.1C

JUNE

1st 1975 Minimum 2.0C

2nd 1953 (Coronation Day) was famously cold, maximum 52F (10.9C)
2nd 1965 Minimum 38F (3.7C)
2nd 1969 Minimum 2.2C
2nd 1975 A fine May had ended with high pressure retreating northwards and a burst of cold NE winds. There was a large reservoir of very cold air in the Arctic north of Iceland. Late on the 1st a polar low formed near Iceland and ran south-eastward.. Under clear skies the thermometer dropped to 2.0C, and as the low neared it produced a heavy shower of sleet and snow
2nd 1989 Record low for June: 0.9C
2nd 1998 Rainfall 34.8mm

3rd 1962 Minimum 36F (2.2C)

5th 1982 Maximum 30.8C
5th 1991 Minimum 1.2C
5th 2012 Jubilee Celebration: record low maximum 9.7C

7th 1950 Maximum 87F (30.6C)

10th 1970 Maximum 30.7C

11th 1969 Minimum 4.1C
11th 1997 Rainfall 34.1mm

12th 1986 Minimum 1.6C
12th 2015 Rainfall 31.0mm

14th 1973 Minimum 2.3C

15th 1971 Minimum 3.8C

18th 1960 Maximum 88F (31.2C), at the time a record high for June
18th 1983 Rainfall 33.1mm

19th 2000 Maximum 33.4C
18th 2005 Maximum 31.8C

20th 1989 Maximum 31.6C

22nd 2007 Rainfall 47.3mm

26th 1976 Hottest June day on record: 34.1C
26th 2001 Maximum 30.6C

28th 1957 Maximum 87F (30.6C)
28th 1981 Minimum 3.7C

29th 1968 Maximum 29.5C

30th 1961 Maximum 86F (30.0C)
30th 1995 Maximum 31.5C

July

1st 1958 Wet day, 1.47ins (37.4mm)
1st 1968 Maximum 32.1C, an isolated hot day after deposits of Saharan sand the previous day
1st 2015 Record July heat reached 35.6C
This was the outstanding day of a poor summer. Britain became sandwiched between high pressure to the west and low pressure approaching from the Atlantic. Weather had become very hot over Spain and France and souteasterly winds briefly fed this hot air into the UK. Temperature peaked at 35.6C: the second hottest day on record

3rd 1967 Minimum 6.6C
3rd 1976 Maximum 33.9C at the end of 8 days all above 30C
3rd 1989 Minimum 6.3C

4th 1965 Minimum 39F (3.9C), record low for July

5th 1959 Maximum 92F (33.3C), during a famously hot summer, a record high at the time
5th Wet day; 46.1mm

7th 1970 Maximum 33.2C

9th 1980 Rainfall 32.4mm

11th 1994 Maximum 32.3C

12th 1972 Minimum 4.1C

15th 1977 Minimum 5.5C

16th 1969 Maximum 33.1C

18th 1959 Minimum 6.6C
18th 1971 Minimum 4.6C

19th 1974 Minimum 6.2C

20th 2007 Deep summer Low produced 38.0mm rain

22nd 1989 Maximum 34.3C
22nd 2004 Wet day; 43.4mm

23rd 1957 Minimum 43F (6.1C), at the time a record low for July
23rd 2013 2hour downpour produced record 66.3mm

28th 1957 Maximum 87F (30.6C)

29th 1975 Maximum 31.5C

30th 2002 Wet day; 32.4mm

31st 1998 Very wet day: 52.4mm
31st 2015 Minimum 5.7C

August

1st 1976 Minimum 4.5C
1st 1995 Maximum 32.1C
1st 2013 Maximum 32.4C

2nd 1984 Rainfall 41.1mm
2nd 1999 Maximum 32.9C

3rd 1990 'Hot Friday' when temperature reached a record 37.0C (98.6F)
High pressure to the east had produced sunny weather with steadily climbing temperatures all week. It culminated in what was for many places the hottest day on record.

8th 1975 Maximum 33.3C hottest on record for August at the time

9th 2004 A record 98.4mm: continuous heavy rain
In a summer of repeated heavy rainstorms, the one which occurred on the 9th August was record breaking. The preceding days had been mostly warm and sunny, then an old hurricane approached winds backed SE on the 8th which reached 29.1C. Rain began to fall at 08h on the 9th and did not finally cease until 12h on the 10th. In that period, 107.8mm rain fell, of which 98.4mm during the 'rainfall day' of the 9th

11th 1997 Maximum 32.3C

12th 1953 Hot day with southerly winds, max 90F (32.2C)

14th 1980 Thunderstorm with 49.1mm rain within 2 hours

16th 1971 Minimum 4.6C

17th 1970 Minimum 5.5C

18th 1996 Maximum 30.6C
18th 2005 Rainfall 30.4mm

19th 1968 Minimum 5.5C,

24th 1966 Minimum 40F (4.4C)

28th 1974 Minimum 5.0C
28th 1979 Minimum 4.1C

31st 1986 Minimum 4.0C, coldest August night

September

1st 1954 Maximum 81F (27.3C); hottest day of the year
1st 1991 Maximum 30.5C; record for September

6th 1989 Maximum 26.7C

7th 1973 Maximum 27.2C

8th 1967 Minimum 2.8C record low at the time

9th 1972 Rainfall 49.3mm; wettest for September

10th 1968 Maximum 26.3C

11th 1999 Maximum 28.8C

12th 1985 Maximum 26.8C

14th 1994 Rainfall 46.3mm

16th 1975 Minimum -0.2C (equal record low for September at the time)

17th 1986 Minimum -1.4C; record low for September

18th 1982 Maximum 28.4C; record high for September at the time

21st 2006 Maximum 26.8C

22nd 1992 Rainfall 31.7mm

24th 1979 Minimum 0.8C

26th 1972 Minimum 0.6C

28th 1970 Maximum 26.2C

29th 1974 Minimum 0.7C

29th 1987 Minimum 1.7C

30th 1969 Minimum -0.2C
30th 2011 Maximum 27.1C
One of the most outstanding spells in the Newark Almanack is the unusual spell of very warm/hot weather that lasted for a week 27 September to 3 October
The unseasonably very warm weather originated as a large High developed over the near Continent, and it was the persistence of this basic set up which resulted in the prolongation of heat even into the early days of October

OCTOBER

1st 1953 Maximum 69F (20.6C)
1st 1985 Maximum 28.6C Record high for October and hottest day in the year.
This was the remarkable coda to an indifferent summer. The last week of September had produced a prolonged Indian Summer with gentle southerly breezes and day maxima of 22-24C. As the high moved away freshening southerly breezes brought air from far south. The day began with an overnight low of 17.0C, and by 08h it had already climbed to 21C. The afternoon maximum was 28.6C- the hottest of the year
1st 1997 Rainfall 27.7mm
1st 2011 Maximum 26.7C (see 30 September)

2nd 1971 Maximum 23.4C

3rd 1959 Maximum 76F (24.4C); record for a time

4th 1965 Maximum 74F (23.3C)
4th 1983 Maximum 21.8C

8th 1979 Maximum 22.0C
8th 1995 Maximum 22.9C

9th 1969 Maximum 22.8C

10th 1970 Minimum -2.2C

11th 1976 Maximum 20.3C

12th 1973 Minimum -1.5C

12th 1978 Maximum 24.8C For time October highest
12th 1990 Maximum 24.3C

16th 1981 Minimum -2.6C

17th 1990 Rainfall 51.4mm

18th 1993 Minimum -2.8C

20th 1980 Minimum -1.6C

22nd 1983 Minimum -2.9C

25th 1979 Rainfall 28.6mm

27th 2012 After a overnight Low of 1.7C, snow fell and briefly settled

29th 1997 Minimum -4.1C, record low for October
29th 2008 Minimum -1.9C

31st 1974 Minimum -0.9C
31st 1988 Minimum -3.1C

November

1st 1977 Rainfall 27.0mm
1st 1983 Maximum 16.6C
1st 1983 Maximum 17.0C
1st 1984 Maximum 16.6C

2nd 1969 Maximum 17.3C; at the time highest in November
2nd 1970 Maximum 16.4C
2nd 1996 Maximum 17.2C
2nd 2005 Record maximum for November 17.5C

3rd 1979 Maximum 16.7C
3rd 1984 Minimum -6.0C

4th 1971 Maximum 16.6C
4th 1978 Maximum 16.5C
4th 2010 Maximum 17.3C

5th 1951 Rainfall 1.30ins (32.5mm)

6th 1972 Maximum 16.3C

8th 1985 Maximum 16.5C

10th 1977 Maximum 16.2C
10th 2015 Maximum 17.2C

11th 1979 Minimum -5.2C
11th 2000 Rainfall 28.4mm

22nd 1983 Minimum -6.0C

22nd 1988 Minimum -6.0C

24th 2010 Rainfall 27.2mm

25th 1952 Minimum 21F (-6.1C)

28th 1973 Minimum -7.0C; at the time coldest in November
28th 2010 Minimum -8.8C, record cold for November
The early part of November 2010 had been mild, but northeasterlies spread across the UK on the 22nd and it became progressively colder. There had been snow early on the 27th leaving a 2cm cover, with further snow showers through the day. As wind fell light and skies cleared, an exceptionally cold night followed, with a record low for November of -8.8C

29th 1969 Minimum -5.9C

30th 1978 Minimum -6.7C

December

1st 1973 Minimum -8.7C
1st 1975 Rainfall 28.6mm

3rd 1960 Rainfall 1.23ins 31.0mm

4th 1976 Minimum -5.2C

5th 1979 Maximum 13.5C

6th 1962 Minimum 20F (-6.7C)

7th 2010 Minimum -12.0C

8th 1957 Maximum 56F (12.8C)

13th 1951 Minimum 22F (-5.6C)
13th 1981 Minimum -12.6C; December cold record

15th 1952 Maximum 56F (12.8C)
15th 1982 Maximum 14.9C long-time December record
15th 2015 Maximum 15.0C, warmest in December

19th 1993 Maximum 13.9C

20th 1967 Minimum -6.2C
20th 1972 Maximum 13.6C
20th 1999 Minimum -6.3C
20th 2014 Maximum 14.0C

22nd 1991 Maximum 13.8C

23rd 1977 Maximum 14.8C

24th 2011 Maximum 13.7C

25th 1962 Minimum 20F (-6.7C)
25th 1992 Minimum -5.8C

26th 1988 Maximum 14.1C

28th 1955 Maximum 57F (13.9C)
28th 1974 Maximum 14.4C;

29th 1961 Minimum 21F (-6.1C)
29th 1995 Minimum -7.2C

30th 1985 Minimum -6.8C

2. LONG-RANGE TEMPERATURES

Comprehensive lists of the outstanding weather events have concentrated on temperature extremes
On the following two pages are data of long-term averages for the sixty-five years covered in this book

LONG-TERM TEMPERATURE* (1951-2015)

	Jan	Feb	Mar	Apr	May	June
Av High	12.1	12.5	15.9	19.6	24.7	27.6
Highest	15.1 9,2015	18.3 23,1990	23.4 29,1965	25.8 23,2011	30.7 23,2010	34.1 26,1976
Av Low	-5.2	-5.7	-2.2	-1.2	1.9	5.2
Lowest	-16.1 13,1987	-10.5 28,1955	-10.0 3,1965	-6.5 20,1968	-2.8 27,1967	0.9 2,1989
Av Max	5.9	6.8	9.9	13.1	17.2	20.7
Av Min	1.7	1.2	2.8	5.2	6.9	10.4
Frosts	8.8	9.7	5.3	2.2	0.3	0
Frost Days	1.2	0.4	0	0	0	0
Warm Days**	0	0	0	0	1.2	4.3

*in degrees Celsius
**Above 25C

LONG-TERM TEMPERATURE* (1951-2015)

	July	Aug	Sep	Oct	Nov	Dec
Av High	27.7	27.9	24	19.6	14.7	12.1
Highest	35.6 1,2015	37 3,1990	30.5 1,1991	28.4 1,1985	17.5 2,2005	15.0 15,2015
Av Low	6.5	7.3	4.4	0.6	-2.7	-4.2
Lowest	4.1 12,1972	4 31,1986	-1.4 17,1986	-4.1 29,1997	-8.8 28,2010	-12.6 13,1981
Av Max	22.3	21.8	18.7	13.9	9.1	6.7
Av Min	12.4	12.2	10.2	7.4	4.1	2.9
Frosts	0	0	0	1	4.3	7.8
Frost Days	0	0	0	0	0.3	0.9
Warm Days**	7.6	5.3	1	0.2	0	0

*in degrees Celsius
**Above 25C

3. RAINFALL

Reliable rainfall data are not available before 1969, so the span of years is just 47. There is also a gap in data for the months of May to December 1993. Data are presented in millimeters. (There are 25.4mm to 1 inch rain.)

Days when snow falls are included in the total: this is standard practice. The snow collected in the gauge is melted and the water thus obtained is the day's total. Rainfall has throughout been measured at 08h and the total credited to the day before (as that represented 2/3 of the day.).

Newark-on-Trent lies in the dry southeastern quarter of the country which is well away the driest.

RAINFALL DATA (1969-2015)

	Average	Wettest	Driest	Rain Days
Jan	49.6	98.4(2014)	10.4(2000)	17
Feb	37.8	147.4(1977)	10.1(1993)	12.8
Mar	41	87.2(1981)	9.0(1990)	13.8
Apr	41.4	145.7(2000)	2.9(2007)	12.5
May*	50.5	119.6(2014)	13.6(1991)	12
June*	61.1	242.7(2007)	7.3(1976)	11.5
July*	59.1	136.8(2007)	7.5(1995)	11.3
Aug*	57.8	183.2(2004)	2.2(1983)	11.9
Sep*	53.1	115.0(1976)	6.2(1986)	11.5
Oct*	53	125.9(2004)	16.1(1975)	14.1
Nov*	53.2	93.2(2002)	19.3(1978)	16.9
Dec*	54.1	146.0(1978)	14.7(1980)	15.6

*No data for 1993

Outstanding Months.

Below are listed the most outstanding rainfall months. We note the months of highest and lowest rainfall total

We note (a) the driest months; all those with a rainfall total below 8.0mm (b) the wettest months. Here we include months with above 120mm

Driest and Wettest Months on record.(mm rain)

Driest	Month	Wettest	Month
2.2	August-1983	242.7	June-2007
4.8	October-1978	183.2	August-2004
5.2	April-2011	180.6	June-1997
6.2	September-1986	151.7	June-1998
6.8	October-1969	146	December-1998
7.3	April-1974	136.8	July-2007
7.3	June-1976	135.9	July-2002
7.5	June-1995	122.8	June-1987

4. FROST AND FOG; HAIL AND THUNDER

Frost

An air frost is recorded when the minimum temperature falls below freezing-point (-0.1C). When the maximum fails to exceed freezing-point, then this is counted as a 'freezing day'. The occurences of both elements are again presented in a month-by-month table.

'Ground Frost' is recorded when a special grass minimum thermometer laid just above the surface of grass falls below freezing-point. Whilst this element was recorded for a few years, these were too few for meaningful data to be given here.

	Jan	Feb	Mar	Apr	May	Sep	Oct	Nov	Dec
Frosts	9	10	5.4	2.3	0.3	0.05	1	4.3	7.8
Freeze Days	1.3	0.4	0	0	0	0	0	1.3	1

Fog

Fog is needless to say another element of weather which causes disruption. Many readers of this book may not have recollection of the old-fashioned 'smog'- so called because it was fog combined with smoke, and with a reduction in smoke from both domestic and industrial sources has eliminated this risk.

Fog, in the meteorological sense is recorded when the visibilty falls below 1000 metres (1 km). Fog becomes a nuisance when it, mainly, makes transport-movement difficult or dangerous. (This author recalls acting as a consultant to the Environment Agency over plans for the route of the by-pass for the A46).

Fog, again, is mainly a fact-of-life in the winter half of the year. During the summer any mist of fog which might form overnight is dispersed readily once the sun is up. It can be a hazard in coastal locations. To record 'fog', visibility of less than 1 km must be observed at 09h.

Observations of 'fog' were not kept until 1971, so we have 40 years of data to work with.

Hail and Thunder

These two elements need no introduction. Both products of an 'unstable' atmosphere they tend to occur together.

We should note however a type of hail known as 'soft hail'. Most hail is the result of frozen rain droplets being carried up and down by air-currents. On each ascent, the frozen drops accrete yet more ice, increasing in weight until finally the updraught can hold them no longer.

Date for fog (1971-2010)

	Days with fog (average)
January	1.1
February	1.4
March	0.6
April	0.2
May	0.05
June	0
July	0.07
August	0.1
September	0.4

October	1.1
November	1.5
December	1.8

One fact that strikes immediately is that there is a correlation between frequency of fog and the length of the night. Fog is reported most frequently in December, with the longest nights, whilst the only fog-free month is June, with the shortest nights

Soft hail is the product of a cold atmosphere.

Data for hail and thunder (1971-2010)

	Days with hail	Days with thunder
January	0.4	0.1
February	0.5	0.1
March	1.3	0.3
April	0.9	0.3
May	0.5	1.2
June	0.3	1.6
July	0.1	1.9
August	0.1	1.8
September	0.05	0.7
October	0.2	0.3
November	0.1	0.05
Dec	0.1	0.1

5. NEWARK-ON-TRENT YEAR-BY-YEAR

1951. Avg max 13.0C, min 6.3C
Year's highest, 26.1C on 1 July/4 August, lowest -5.6C on 13 December Highest minimum 17.2C on 4 August, lowest maximum -0.6C on 29 January.

1952. Avg max 13.2C, min 6.3C
Year's highest, 28.9C on 28,30 June, lowest -7.2C on 27 January. Highest minimum 19.4C on 1 July, lowest maximum 0.0C on 27 January.

1953 Avg max 13.9C, min 7.1C
Year's highest 32.2C on 12 August, lowest -3.3C on 8 February/5 March. Highest minimum 18.9C on 13 August, lowest maximum 0.6C on 19 January.

1954. Avg max 13.3C, min 6.5C
Year's highest 27.2C on 1 September, lowest -7.8C on 4 February.Highest minimum 16.7C on 4 July, lowest maximum -1.1C on 28 January/1 February. (Highest up to 31 August only 25.5C, redeemed on 1 Sept.)

1955. Avg max 13.5C, min 6.3C
Year's highest 27.8C on 27/28 July, lowest -10.6C on 28 February. Highest minimum 18.9C on 18 July, lowest maximum -0.6C on 17 January. (A cold winter prolonged into March- avg max 6.9C, min 0.1C)

1956. Avg max 12.8C min 6.0C.
Year's highest 26.1C on 8 July, lowest -8.9C on 2 February. Highest minimum 16.1C on 9,24 July, lowest maximum -2.2C on 1,2 February (poorest summer for the 60 years)

1957. Avg max 13.9C, min 7.1C
Year's highest 30.6C on 28 June, lowest -3.3C on 20 February/8 December. Highest minimum 17.2C on 7 July, lowest maximum 1.7C on 16 December.

1958 Avg max 13.3C, min 6.8C
Year's highest 26.7C on 10 August, lowest -6.1C on 24 January. Highest minimum 16.7C on 6 September, lowest maximum -0.6C on 24 January.

1959. Avg max 15.0C, min 7.0C
Year's highest 33.3C on 5 July, lowest -5.6C on 11,16 January. Highest minimum 18.3C on 25 August, lowest maximum -1.1C on 14,16 January
Summer was one of the best, amidst many poor ones.

1960. Avg max 13.8C, 7.0C
Year's highest 31.1C on 18 June, lowest -4.4C on 14 January, Highest minimum 17.2C on 18 June, lowest minimum 1.1C on 13,14 January.

1961 Avg max 14.1C min 6.8C
Year's highest 30.0C on 30 June, lowest -6.1C on 25,29 December, Highest minimum 16.7C on 16 September, lowest maximum -1.7C on 28 December. (Very mild Feb/March: frost free, March highs up to 18C)

1962. Avg max 12.6C min 5.6C
Year's highest 26.1C on 9 June, lowest -9.4C on 3 January. Highest minimum 16.7C on 20 August, lowest maximum -1.7C on 25,29 December

1963 Avg max 12.5C, min 5.7C
Year's highest 27.8C on 12 June, lowest -11.7C on 23 January. Highest minimum 16.7C on 24 July, lowest maximum -6.1C on 24 January (Coldest winter for Britain since 1740)

1964 Avg max 13.5C, min 6.8C
Year's highest 28.3C on 26 August, lowest -6.7C on 29 December.
Highest minimum 17.2C on 26 July/2 August, lowest maximum -1.7C
on 16 December.

1965 Avg max 13.3C, min 5.7C
Year's highest 29.4C on 14 May, lowest -10.0C on 3 March.
Highest minimum 15.6C on 13 June, lowest maximum -1.7C on 28
December (Year's maximum on 14 May)

1966. Avg max 13.4C, min 6.0C
Year's highest 27.8C on 17,19 August, lowest -7.8C on 19
January. Highest minimum 17.8C on 12 August, lowest maximum
-1.1C on 19 January.

1967 Avg max 13.2C, min 5.8C
Year's highest 31.1C on 17 July, lowest -6.9C on 9 January.
Highest minimum 17.0C on 17 July, lowest maximum -0.9C on 20
December

1968 Avg max 13.5C, min 5.6C
Year's highest 33.0C on 1 July, lowest -8.8C on 10 January.
Highest minimum 15.0C on 1,15 July, lowest maximum -1.0C on 10
January

1969 Avg max 12.9C min 5.4C
Year's highest 33.1C on 16 July, lowest -10.4C on 8 February.
Highest minimum 16.6C on 10 August, lowest maximum -1.0C on 16
February (very wintry Feb with avg max 2.3C, min -2.2C   20 frosts,
13 days with snow)

1970 Avg max 13.8C min 5.7C
Year's highest 33.2C on 7 July, lowest -9.9C on 7 January.
Highest minimum 16.8C on 8 July, lowest maximum -2.6C on 7
January. Rain
597.4mm on 167 days

1971 Avg max 13.8C, min 5.7C
Year's highest 29.5C on 30 June, lowest -8.2C on 5 January.
Highest minimum 16.0C on 24 July, lowest maximum -3.3C on 3
January Rain 562.3mm on 149 days. Wettest 46.1mm on 5 July.

1972. Avg max 13.2C, min 5.5C
Year's highest 27.0C on 20 July, lowest -10.2C on 31 January.
Highest minimum 14.8C on 7 August, lowest maximum -2.9C on 31
January Rain 593.7mm on 168 days. Wettest 47.8mm on 9 September

1973 Avg max 14.0C, min 5.8C
Year's highest 30.4C on 16 August, lowest -8.7C on 3 December.
Highest minimum 16.5C on 15 August, lowest maximum -0.5C on 18
January. Rain 486.1mm on 128 days. Wettest 47.2mm on 19 June

1974 Avg max 13.7C, min 5.9C
Year's highest 25.8C 20 June, lowest -6.7C on 1 January. Highest
minimum 15.9C on 20 July, lowest maximum -0.7C on 2 January. Rain
583.3mm on 164 days. Wettest 24.3mm on 4 July.

1975 Avg max 14.7C, min 5.9C
Year's highest 33.3C on 8 August, lowest -4.1C on 14 November.
Highest minimum 18.0C on 5 August, lowest maximum -0.5C on 30
November, Rain 438.3mm on 155 days, Wettest 24.6mm on 4
December.
16 snow days.

1976 Avg max 14.7C, min 5.9C
Year's highest 34.1C on 26 June, lowest -5.2C on 4,5 December.
Highest minimum 17.7C on 19 July, lowest maximum -0.2C on 5
December. Rain 470.6mm on 143 days, wettest 25.8mm on 24
September 20 snow days. (S8mmer of the Century, lasted into
October with six days over 21C (70F))

1977. Avg max 13.5C, min 5.8C
Year's highest 28.9C on 1 August, lowest -5.6C on 30 January.

Highest minimum 16.5C on 23 July, lowest maximum -0.5C on 12 January. Rain 645.6mm on 167 days. Wettest 27.0mm on 1 November. 30 snow days.

1978 Avg max 13.2C, min 5.8C
Year's highest 29.2C on 1 June, lowest -7.4C on 1 December, Highest minimum 16.8C on 10 September, Lowest maximum -3.2C on 30 November. Rain 658.4mm on 161 days. Wettest 26.9mm on 13 August 36 snow days. (Very mild November ended with severe frost on 30th)

1979 Avg max 12.8C min 5.2C
Year's highest 28.3C on 27 July, lowest -12.2C on 28 January. Highest minimum 16.1C on 18 July, lowest maximum -3.0C on 1 January. Rain 643.8mm on 179 days. Wettest 49.1mm on 14 August, 44 snow days (very cold first three months)

1980 Avg max 13.2C, min 5.7C
Year's highest 27.7C on 4 June, lowest -6.6C on 14 January. Highest minimum 15.9C on 15 August, lowest maximum -0.1C on 18 January. Rain 674.4 on 163 days. Wettest 49.1mm on 14 August. 18 snow days.

1981 Avg max 13.2C, min 5,5C
Year's highest 28.2C on 4,17 August, lowest -12.6C on 13 December. Highest minimum 19.3C on 9 July, lowest maximum -5.8C on 17 December. Rain 610.1mm on 178 days. 33 snow days (Coldest recorded December)

1982 Avg max 14.2C, min 6.0C
Year's highest 30.2C on 3 August, lowest -14.0C on 14 January Hgihest minimum 17.2C on 8 July, lowest maximum -4.4C on 14 January Rain 571.6mm on 158 days. Wettest 33.1mm on 22 June. 18 snow days.

1983 Avg max 14.8C, min 6.4C
Year's highest 31.7C on 15 July, lowest -6.2C on 4 February.

Highest minimum 19.2C on 20 July, lowest maximum 0.8C on
10,19 February, Rain 523.5mm on 161 days, Wettest 523.5mm on 26
November. 20 snow days.

1984. Avg max 14.0C, min 6.2C
Year's highest 30.8C on 8 July, lowest -5.8C on 25 January.
Highest minimum 17.0C on 2 July, lowest maximum -1.3C on 27
December. Rain 665.3mm on 164 days. Wettest 44.1mm on 2 August.
20 snow days

1985. Avg max 13.4C, min 5.7C
Year's highest 28.6C on 1 October, lowest -9.9C on 17 January.
Highest minimum 18.0C on 30 July, lowest maximum -5.4C on 17
January. Rain 412.9mm on 172 days, wettest 26.1mm on 14 May. 32
snow days. (record heat on 1 October)

1986. Ave max 13.2C, min 5.0C
Year's highest 29.8C on 15 July, lowest -10.1C on 10 February.
Highest minimum 15.7C on 17 June/ 16 July. Lowest maximum -1.8C
on 20 February. Rain 575.6mm on 174 days. Wettest 26.1mm on 25
August, 33 snow days.

1987. Ave max 13.2C, min 5.5C
Year's highest 28.6C on 20 August, lowest -16.1C on 13 January.
Highest minimum 18.1C on 29 June, lowest maximum -4.8C on 12
January, Rain 700.1mm on 169 days, wettest 30.7mm on 22 August.
25 snow days. (Record low on 13th actually occurred at about 20h on
12th)
1988. Ave max 14.1C, min 6.3C
Year's highest 30.4C on 7 August, lowest -5.0C on 22 November.
Highest minimum 16.8C on 22 July, lowest maximum 2.9C on 21

November .Rain 591.5mm on 153 days, wettest 26.8mm on 20 July. 9 snow days.

1989 Ave max 15.4C, min 6.4C
Year's highest 34.3C on 22 July, lowest -3.5 on 17 February.

Highest minimum 16.5C on 23 July, lowest maximum 0.8C on 27 November. Rain 550.3mm on 145 days, wettest 34.9mm on 30 June. 11 snow days.

1990 Ave max 15.6C, min 6.9C
Year's highest 37.0C on 3 August, lowest -5.1C on 5 April. Highest minimum 18.9C on 24 August, lowest maximum 1.5C on 8 December. Rain 559.8mm on 148 days, wettest 51.4mm on 17 October. 7 snow days.

1991 Ave max 14.2C, min 6.0C
Year's highest 30.5C on 1 September, lowest -10.0C on 14 February. Highest minimum 18.4C on 10 August , lowest maximum -2.7C on 12 December. Rain 430.7mm on 134 days, wettest 27.9mm on 28 September. 5 snow days.

1992 Ave max 14.3C, min 6.4C
Year's highest 30.8C on 29 June, lowest -6.7C on 22 January. Highest minimum 16.6C on 30 June, lowest maximum -2.2C on 29 December. Rain 644.4mm on 169 days. Wettest 31.0mm on 22 September, 5 snow days

1993 Ave max 13.4C, min 6.0C
Year's highest 28.1C on 9 June, lowest -6.0C on 3 January. Highest minimum 15.5C on 16 July/20 August. Lowest maximum -0.9C on 2 January. 14 snow days

1994 Ave max 14.0C, Min 6.7C
Year's highest 32.2C on 11 July, lowest -6.3C on 22 February.

Highest minimum 18.0C on 27 July/5 August. Lowest maximum -1.3C on 23 December. Rain 596.4mm on 159 days, wettest 46.3mm on 14 September 12 snow days.

1995. Ave max 14.5C, Min 6.7C
Year's highest 32.2C on 1 August, lowest -7.2C on 29 December. Highest minimum 20.3C on 30 July, lowest maximum -3.0C on 28

December. Rain 475.4mm on 144 days, wettest 27.9mm on 10 September. 14 snow days.

1996. Ave max 13.1C, min 5.6C
Year's highest 31.6C on 22 July, lowest -5.1C on 26 December. Highest minimum 17.6C on 14 July, lowest maximum -1.1C on 27 January. Rain 485.8mm on 148 days, wettest 27.3mm on 19 Dec. 20 snow days.

1997 Ave max 14.8C, min 6.9C
Year's highest 32.8C on 11 August, lowest -7.7C on 3 January. Highest minimum 19.0C on 13 August, lowest maximum -0.1C on 3 January. Rain 641.8mm on 151 days, wettest 39.4mm on 11 June. 10 snow days.
1998 Ave max 13.9C, min 6.9C
Year's highest 28.7C on 10 August, lowest -3.8C on 28 January. Highest minimum 17.7C on 21 June, lowest maximum 1.3C on 21 December. Rain 809.2mm on 175 days, wettest 51.4mm on 31 July. 7 snow days

1999. Ave max 14.4C, min 8.0C
Year's highest 32.9C on 2 August, lowest -6.3C on 20 December. Highest minimum 18.7C on 3 August, lowest maximum -1.4C on 20 December. Rain 704.7mm on 168 days, wettest 52.7mm on 25 August. 11 snow days.

2000 Ave max 14.0C, min 7.3C
Year's highest 33.4C on 19 June, lowest -3.1C on 31 December.
Highest minimum 17.7C on 3 August, lowest maximum 0.1C on 28
December. Rain 839.2mm on 170 days, wettest 28.4mm on 11
November. 5 snow days. (very wet autumn with severe flooding in
November.)

2001. Ave max 13.9C, min 7.5C
Year's highest 31.1C on 15 August, lowest -5.1C on 18
January.Highest minimum 20.9C on 3 July, lowest maximum -1.0C on
17 January. Rain 651.4mm on 153 days, wettest 23.9mm on 14 May.
17 snow days.

2002. Ave max 14.8C, min 7.9C
Year's highest 29.8C on 17 August, lowest -6.6C on 2 January.
Highest minimum 18.4C on 30 July, lowest maximum 1.2C on 4
January. Rain 724.8mm on 166 days, wettest 35.3mm on 30 July. 3
snow days.

2003. Ave max 14.7C, min 7.5C
Year's highest 30,3C on 9 August, lowest -3.8C on 31
December.Highest minimum 19.0C on 10 August. Lowest maximum
1.2C on 30 December. Rain 475.9mm on 132 days, wettest 24.8mm on
22 June. 10 snow days. (missed ou on the records highs reached
further south)

2004 Ave max 14.4C, min 8.0C
Year's highest 29.5C on 8 June, lowest -2.5C on 2,3,20
December. Highest minimum 21.9C on 9 August. Lowest maximum
1.5C on 25 February. Rain 751.8mm on 172 days, wettest 98.4mm on
9 August. 11 snow days.

2005 Ave max 14.5C, min 7.7C
Year's highest 31.8C on 19 June, lowest -3.9 on 19 November.
Highest minimum 18.3C on 20 June, lowest maximum -1.1C on 30
December. Rain 578.7mm on 148 days, wettest 30.7mm on 18 August.
16 snow days

2006. Ave max 14.9C, min 8.3C
Year's highest 31.8C on 19 June, lowest -5,1 on 3 March. Highest minimum 18.7C on 22 July, lowest maximum -1.9C on 30 December. Rain 627.8mm on 157 days, wettest 33.0mm on 22 July. 9 snow days.

2007 Ave max 14.6C, min 7.8C
Year's highest 28.8C on 5 August, lowest -4.4C on 7 February. Highest minimum 17.6C on 4 August, lowest maximum 1.5C on 14 December. Rain 785.2mm on 152 days, wettest 47.9mm on 22 June. 5 snow days

2008 Ave max 14.5C, min 7.4C
Year's highest 31.3C on27 July, lowest -5.0C on 18 February. Highest minimum 18.9C on 27 July/30 August, lowest maximum -0.5C on 31 December. Rain 634.3mm on 159 days, wettest 25.0mm on 5 September, 8 snow days.

2009 Ave max 14.8C, min 7.4C
Year's highest 31.5C on 1 July, lowest -5.7C on 20 December. Highest minimum 18.5C on 1 July, lowest maximum 0.1C on 10 January. Rain 572.0mm on 166 days, wettest 25.7mm on 7 June. 15 snow days

2010 Ave max 13.5C, min 6.9C
Year's highest 30.7C on 22 May, lowest -12.0C on 7 December. Highest minimum 20.0C on 2 July, lowest maximum -4.1C on 20 December. Rain 533.5mm on 160 days, wettest 23.4mm on 23 September. 33 snow days.

2011 Ave max 15.3C, min 8.4C
Year's highest 31.17C on 27 June, lowest -4.7C on 21 January Highest minimum 19.3C on 27 June, lowest maximum 1.1C on 21 January. Rain 454.0mm on 121 days, wettest 21.8mm on 21 August. 4 snow days

2012 Ave max 13.7C min 7.3C
Year's highest 30.4C on 28 May, lowest -10.1C on 11 February
Highest minimum 18.7C on 25 July, lowest maximum -0.8C on 11
February. Rain 867.6mm on 176 days, wettest, 27.2mm on 27
November. 6 snow days

2013 Ave max 13.8C min 7.3C
Year's highest 32.4C on 1 August, lowest ,-5.9C on 17 January
Highest minimum 19.2C on 20 July, lowest maximum -2.4C on 16
January. Rain 616.7mm on 146 days, wettest 66.9mm on 23 July. 28
snow days.

2014 Ave max 15.0C min 8.7C
Year's highest 31.3C on 26 July, lowest -3.0C on 29 December
Highest minimum 19.5C on 19 July lowest maximum 1.3C on 30
December. Rain 727.9mm on 177 days wettest 25.7mm on 10 August
5 snow days.

2015 Ave max 14.4C min 7.7C
Year's highest 35.6C on 1 July, lowest -3.1C on 4 January
Highest minimum 17.7C on 10 August, lowest maximum 1.9C on 4
January. Rain `574.1mm on 160 days, wettest 31.0mm on 12 May
4 snow days

6. CLIMATIC TRENDS
(short- and long-term)

Climatologists now accept that our climate is warming world-wide. What is the evidence in the Newark record? The two graphs below illustrate the year-on-year records: the first graph for rainfall from 1956 through to 2005; the latter the temperature record from 1956 to 2005(shown in red). In both cases the trends are more clearly seen by the 9-year-centred moving means (shown in green)

The rainfall is shown first. It is often said that for the UK warming will also mean increased rainfall. The 9-year centred data show random year-to-year factors at play until the early 1990s, since when there has been a steady rise by 8 percent

Undoubtedly temperature has also increased during the last 20 years.. The facts, as presented graphically speak for themselves.

There are also suggestions that seasonal patterns may be changing in response to global warming. There have been marked fluctuations to the seasonal distribution of rainfall, with the first five months (except April) showing reduced rainfall, but from June on a marked increase.

Illustrations (below) are based on data prepared in 2009. Note that 2010 was the coldest year since 1986, and there are suggestions that warming may be slowing down in our part of the world.

We see, then, that climatic warming has been very much a factor of the last two decades. These have been decades of, mainly, very mild winters, and summers which, if not always fine and sunny have at least been mild. Thus, we have already noted the fact that the 'poor' summer of 2007 was in fact warm.

The weather of 2010 has caused many to stop and pause and think on the subject of global warming. Not least have been the last three winters. After an unremarkable December and January in 2007-8, bitterly cold easterly winds swept in from Siberia at the end of January and this very cold and snowy weather lasted through to mid-February. It was long enough since, even in the collective memory, we had experienced a sustained spell of cold, snow and the attendant disruption. Just a blip maybe?

Then we had a rude shock. A week before Christmas 2009 we again experienced an incursion of cold north-easterlies with snow causing disruption. Again it lasted, and just when a thaw seemed to be setting in in the New Year, northerly winds brought more snow and frost; this lasted most of January. February was about normal, but with unwanted reminders of cold and snow. Even earlier, it all happened again in late November 2010, and we had one of the coldest Decembers on record.

Is something significant happening...? Too early to tell yet, but theories based on a decline in the Gulf Stream come to mind. On the other hand, although some wintry weather has occurred in February 2012 and February/March 2013, mild winters seem to be 'on track' again. As I write this we have just had a blast of northerly winds, which have not been as cold as one would expect. Is this on account of the warming of the Arctic and retreat of ice?

It is also to be noted that even at the decadal level, climatic change is a more variable factor. The table below lists mean annual temperature for each of the six decades covered by this book.

Decade	Decadal Avg Mean
1951-60	10.1
1961-70	9.6
1971-80	9.7
1981-90	10
1991-2000	10.3
2001-10	11.1

See below for the graphic representation

Temperature 1956-2005

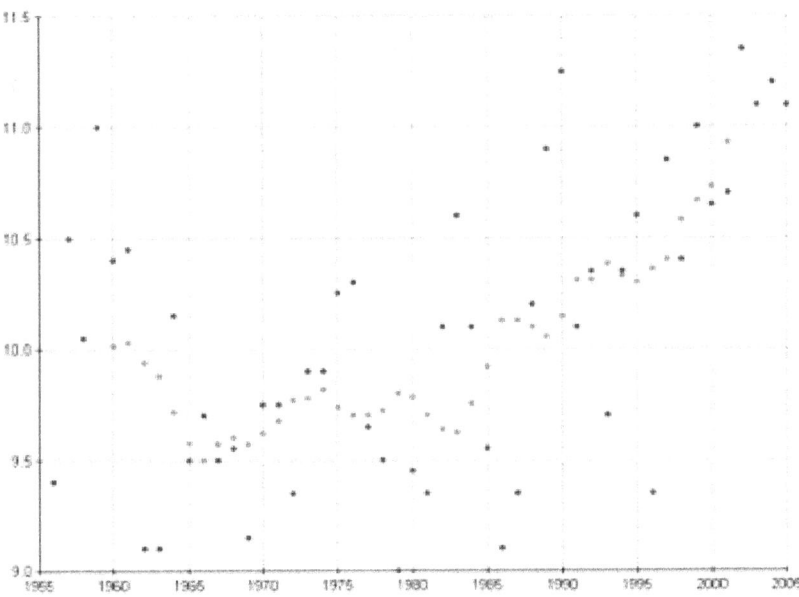

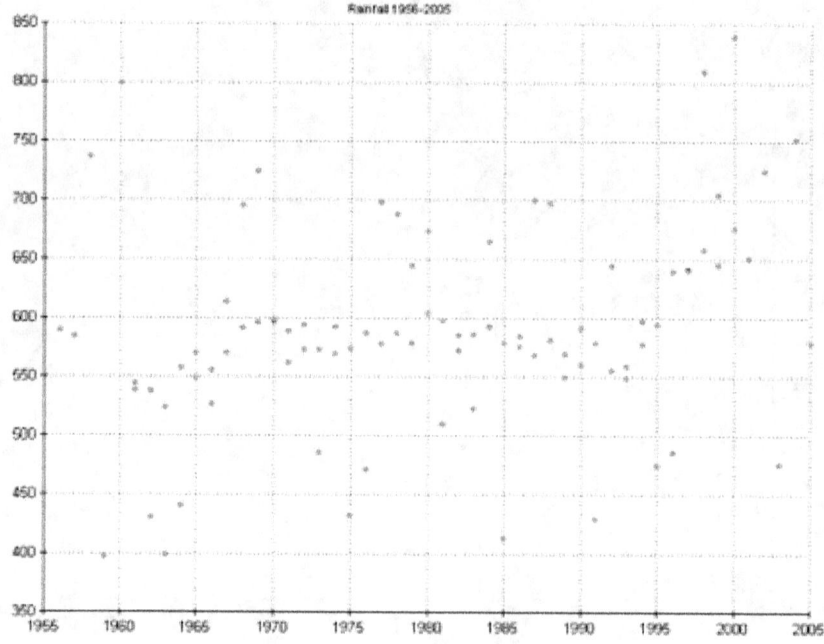

Rainfall 1956-2005

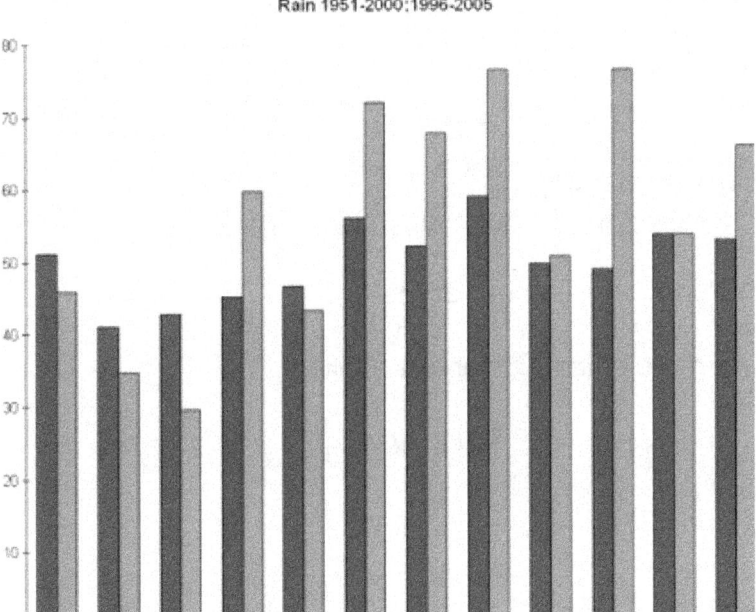

Rain 1951-2000:1996-2005

Useful Websites

http://newarkweather.lyall-web.co.uk/mobile/
(my Newark-on-Trent weather website)
http://uk.weather.com/weather/almanac-UKXX0887
(almanac-Newark)
http://ec.europa.eu/clima/sites/campaign/what/climatechange_en.htm
(climate change)
http://www.weatheronline.co.uk/reports/philip-eden/Coronation-Weather.htm
(Coronation weather 1953)
http://www.colweather.org.uk/
(COL-Climatological Observers' Link)

ALSO BY IAN LYALL
published by lulu.com
available from Amazon

Newark: Six Decades
of Weather

Ian Lyall

ISBN 978-1446788417